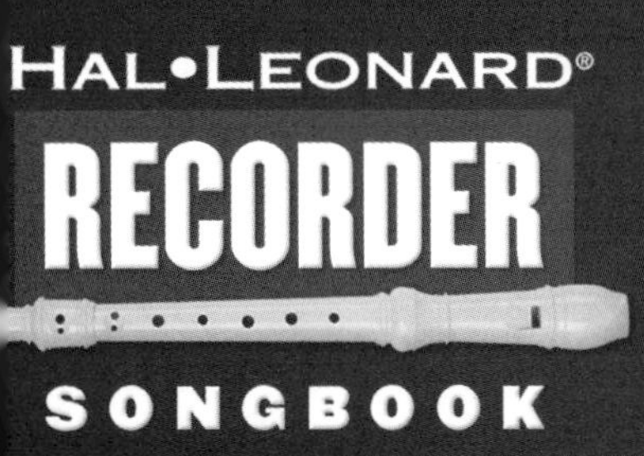

Christmas Songs

CONTENTS

ISBN 978-1-4803-4608-6

7777 W. BLUEMOUND RD. P.O. BOX 13819 MILWAUKEE, WI 53213

Visit Hal Leonard Online at
www.halleonard.com

ALL I WANT FOR CHRISTMAS IS MY TWO FRONT TEETH

RECORDER

Words and Music by
DON GARDNER

CAROLING, CAROLING

RECORDER

Words by WIHLA HUTSON
Music by ALFRED BURT

THE CHRISTMAS SONG
(Chestnuts Roasting on an Open Fire)

RECORDER

Music and Lyric by MEL TORMÉ
and ROBERT WELLS

HAVE YOURSELF A MERRY LITTLE CHRISTMAS

RECORDER

Words and Music by HUGH MARTIN
and RALPH BLANE

A HOLLY JOLLY CHRISTMAS

RECORDER

Music and Lyrics by
JOHNNY MARKS

I HEARD THE BELLS ON CHRISTMAS DAY

RECORDER

Words by HENRY WADSWORTH LONGFELLOW
Adapted by JOHNNY MARKS
Music by JOHNNY MARKS

I'LL BE HOME FOR CHRISTMAS

RECORDER

Words and Music by KIM GANNON
and WALTER KENT

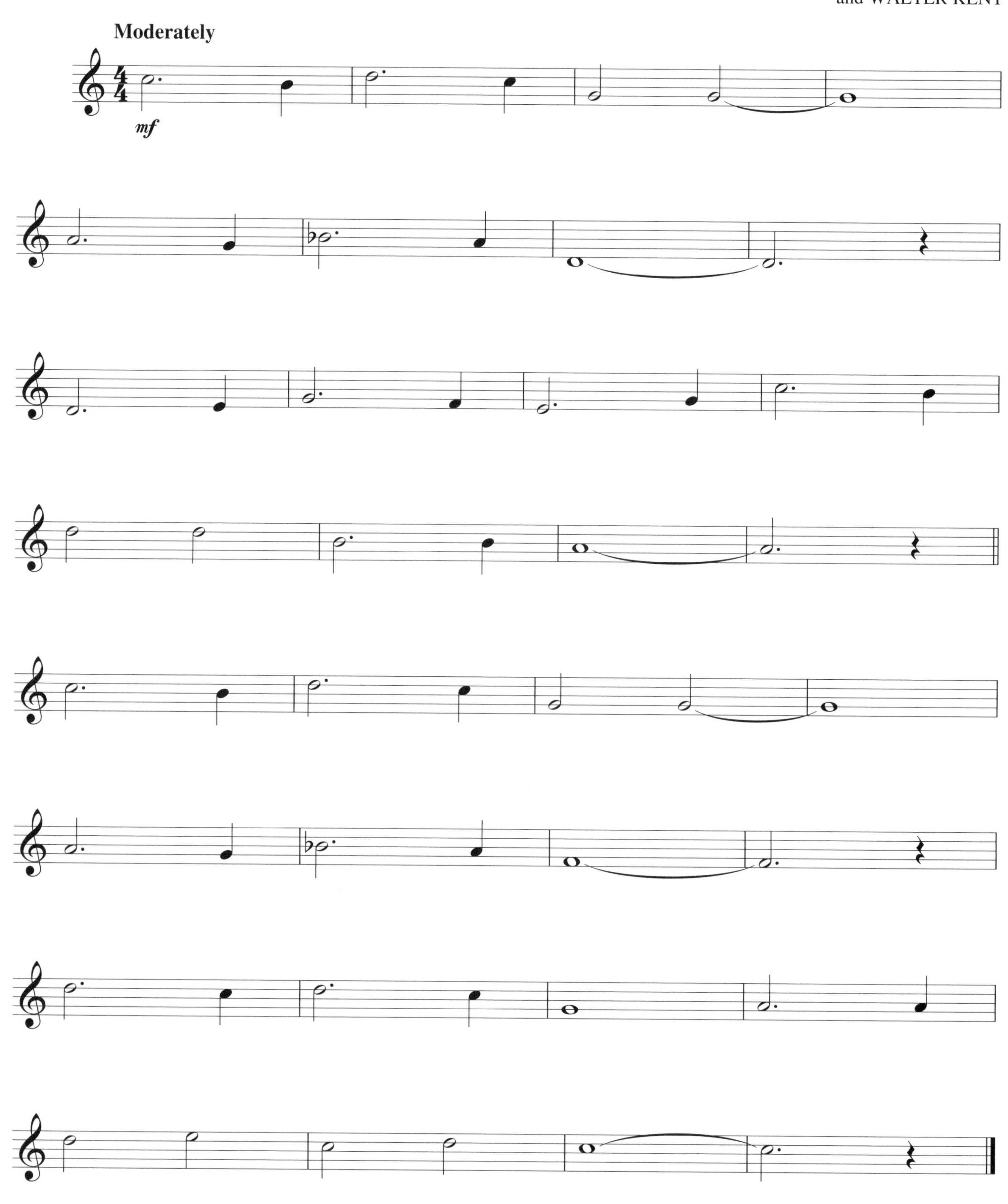

LET IT SNOW! LET IT SNOW! LET IT SNOW!

RECORDER

Words by SAMMY CAHN
Music by JULE STYNE

MERRY CHRISTMAS, DARLING

RECORDER

Words and Music by RICHARD CARPENTER
and FRANK POOLER

THE MOST WONDERFUL TIME OF THE YEAR

ROCKIN' AROUND THE CHRISTMAS TREE

RECORDER

Words and Music by
JOHNNY MARKS

RUDOLPH THE RED-NOSED REINDEER

RECORDER

Music and Lyrics by
JOHNNY MARKS

SANTA CLAUS IS COMIN' TO TOWN

RECORDER

Words by HAVEN GILLESPIE
Music by J. FRED COOTS

SILVER BELLS

from the Paramount Picture THE LEMON DROP KID

RECORDER

Words and Music by JAY LIVINGSTON
and RAY EVANS

WE NEED A LITTLE CHRISTMAS

from MAME

RECORDER

Music and Lyric by
JERRY HERMAN